D1062551

700
L

14.50
96/97

Creativity Around the World

DEMCO

LAINGSBURG
ELEMENTARY LIBRARY

We All Share

CREATIVITY
AROUND THE WORLD

BY

PATRICIA LAKIN

A BLACKBIRCH PRESS BOOK

WOODBRIDGE, CONNECTICUT

CONTENTS

Published by Blackbirch Press, Inc.
One Bradley Road
Woodbridge, CT 06525

©1995 Blackbirch Press, Inc.
First Edition

All rights reserved. No part of this book may be reproduced in any form without permission in writing from Blackbirch Press, Inc., except by a reviewer.

10 9 8 7 6 5 4 3 2 1

Photo Credits
Cover: ©Jeanne Heiberg/Peter Arnold, Inc.; Series Logo: ©Tanya Stone; p.3: Leo de Wys; p. 5: ©Bob Krist/Tony Stone Worldwide, Ltd.; p. 7: ©John C. Stevenson/Peter Arnold, Inc.; p. 9: ©Jose Dupont/Explorer/Photo Researchers, Inc.; p. 11: ©Erika Stone/Peter Arnold, Inc.; p. 13: ©Horst Schafer/Peter Arnold, Inc.; p. 15: Peter Arnold, Inc.; p. 17: ©Jeff Greenberg/Peter Arnold, Inc.; p. 19: ©Fred Bruemmer/ Peter Arnold, Inc.; p. 21: ©Suzanne Murphy/DDB Stock Photo; p. 23: ©D.E. Cox/ Tony Stone Worldwide; p. 25: ©Luiz C. Marigo/Peter Arnold, Inc.; p. 27: Kenya Tourist Office, New York; p. 29: ©Brian Stablyk/Tony Stone Images; p. 31: ©Louis Goldman/Photo Researchers, Inc.

Library of Congress Cataloging–in–Publication Data
Lakin, Pat.
    Creativity / by Patricia Lakin.   —1st ed.
        p.   cm.—(We all share)
    Includes bibliographical references (p.   ) and index.
        ISBN 1–56711–142-4 (alk. paper)
        1. Arts—Juvenile literature. [1. Arts.]   I. Title.
    II. Series.
    NX633.L35   1995
    700–dc20
                                94–41207
                                    CIP
                                    AC

INTRODUCTION

The urge to be creative is part of every human being. How that creativity is shown, however, is different from one person to the next. Some people paint, other people write music. Some people dance, others weave and sew. No matter how they show it, being creative is part of being alive.

In its own way, each country is like one huge family. Countries have rich histories filled with a variety of prized works created by their most famous artists. Today, in every country, there are a wide range of artists creating many wonderful things. Perhaps their plays, dances, songs, pottery, sculpture, or drawings are closely related to their country's ancient art. Or, perhaps their creations are unique and brand new.

In this book, only one art form is selected for mention in each country. In most cases, the art form that was chosen is one that is commonly linked to that country. It is important to remember, however, that each country has many different art forms and a wealth of artists.

A young Chinese teenager puts the finishing touches on a colorful pot.

RUSSIA

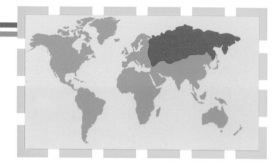

Russia is an immense country whose citizens have a variety of cultures and backgrounds. Many who live in this country are devoted to music and dance, especially ballet and the music that is a part of it.

Ballet was first created in France many years ago. That is why ballet dance steps all have French names. The Russians developed a special love of this type of dancing. Some of the greatest ballet dancers in the world, both male and female, have been Russian. And many world famous dance creators, as well as composers of ballet music, were or are Russian.

Right: Young girls in St. Petersburg wait backstage at the Kirov during a ballet performance.

Russians often encourage their children to study ballet. Talented youngsters are sent to special schools to train for the country's many world-famous ballet companies, such as the Kirov and the Bolshoi.

IRAN

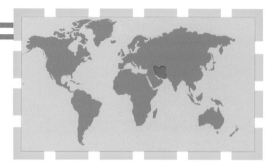

Iran is a Middle Eastern country with an ancient heritage. For many Iranians—and others who live in this part of the world—it is the custom to sit on a prized hand-woven rug or carpet during meals, or while being social.

Iran was once known as Persia. Its world-famous rugs and carpets still carry that name. A Persian rug is made from woolen yarn and silk that is dyed in a variety of beautiful colors. It is also woven by hand on a loom. Persian rugs and carpets come in various rectangular sizes. Most of them are multi-colored and have very bright, complex designs. Some rug or carpet designs are so complicated that they can take a weaver many years to finish.

Right: A rug merchant sits with his goods at an open-air bazaar in Iran.
Inset: A weaver in Shiraz, Iran, works on a rug.

BELGIUM

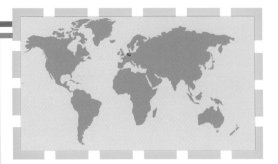

Belgium is a very small European country that borders France, Luxembourg, and the Netherlands. It is known for wonderful chocolate and for its fine, handmade lace.

Lace is a delicate, open fabric made from thin linen threads. It can be sewn onto other material as decoration, or it can be used in large pieces as a tablecloth or bedspread.

Lace can be made in many ways. Bobbin lace is the name of lace made by one process. It is the most common type of lace in many parts of Belgium.

Bobbin lace is also called pillow lace because the work is actually done on a pillow. First, the pattern for the lace is drawn onto thin tissue paper or parchment. The parchment is then placed onto a pillow that the lacemaker rests on his or her lap. Pins are pushed through the parchment paper and into the pillow. Linen thread from bobbins, or spools, is wrapped and tied around the many pins creating the lace pattern. Once the design is completed, the pins are removed and the lace is done.

Beautiful lace patterns are created by tying fine linen thread around a series of pins.

UNITED STATES

The United States of America has a population made up of Native Americans and immigrants from many different countries.

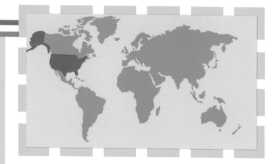

Immigrants brought many things with them when they first arrived on America's eastern shores. Quilts were brought by the Dutch and English colonists in the 1600s. These thick quilts were used as blankets or bedspreads. They kept the colonists warm during the cold, harsh New England winters.

As white Americans moved west, families took their quilts and quilt-making materials with them. Quilting "bees" became popular. These bees were productive social hours where young girls and women would make a quilt together. (Quilting bees are still popular in some parts of the country today.) In pioneer days, women and young girls would sit around a large wooden frame. The frame held the three layers of fabric in place while the workers sewed the quilt.

There are two main types of quilts. A pieced quilt is made from small pieces of fabric that are sewn together to make a larger piece. This is then used for the top cloth of the quilt. An applique quilt has cut-out pieces of fabric that are sewn onto the quilt to make a picture or a design. These designs often show a story in a family's history. Some designs are handed down in families from one generation to another.

An Amish man and woman work on a quilt in Pennsylvania.

GREECE

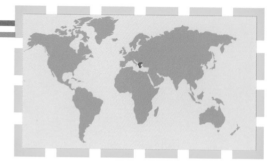

Greece is a small country that lies on the Mediterranean Sea. Some of Greece is on the European mainland. Much of the country, however, is made up of over 2,000 islands off the mainland.

Greece is known for its knitting and weaving of wool. For thousands of years, Greek weavers have created clothes based on traditional patterns and designs.

The hills and pastures all over Greece are dotted with sheep. In fact, sheep are probably the most important animals raised in Greece. In addition to wool, sheep provide the Greek people with many other products. The typical Greek diet includes many foods made from sheep's milk and the meat of sheep, called lamb.

A mother and son tend their woolen crafts shop on the island of Corfu.

The wool from these animals has traditionally been used to create wonderful sweaters, socks, and rugs. Small crafts shops throughout the islands are filled with colorful handwoven wool products for sale.

NAVAJO

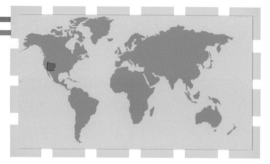

The Navajo—or Diné, as they are also called—are the largest group of Native Americans in the United States. The great majority of Diné today live in the American Southwest, in the states of Arizona, Utah, Colorado, and New Mexico.

Weaving has become a major art form for many Diné. Borrowing traditional designs and shapes from their ancient heritage, the Diné weave beautifully patterned rugs and blankets. With bright, earthy tones that reflect the colors of the American Southwest, these weavers continue a remarkable craft that has been handed down from generation to generation.

Right: A Navajo blanket weaver sits among many of her creations as she works on her loom.

MEXICO

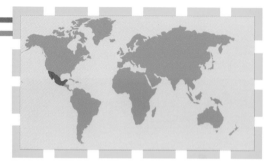

Mexico has a rich mix of Latin American cultures from Central and South America. One population, the Mayans, are an ancient people who have inhabited the area for thousands of years.

As a way of honoring nature, the Mayan people of Mexico weave brightly colored cloth. For the Mayans, who were an early people of this land, using this cloth for their clothing is a very important part of their culture.

The cloth is woven on a special loom, much the same way as it was hundreds of years ago. The designs can have a great deal of meaning because each design identifies the wearer's village. In some

Mayan villages, the designs are even used to tell something about the person wearing the clothes. Some designs tell whether the wearer is married and if he or she has children.

A group of Mayan students sew individual patterns with brightly colored thread.

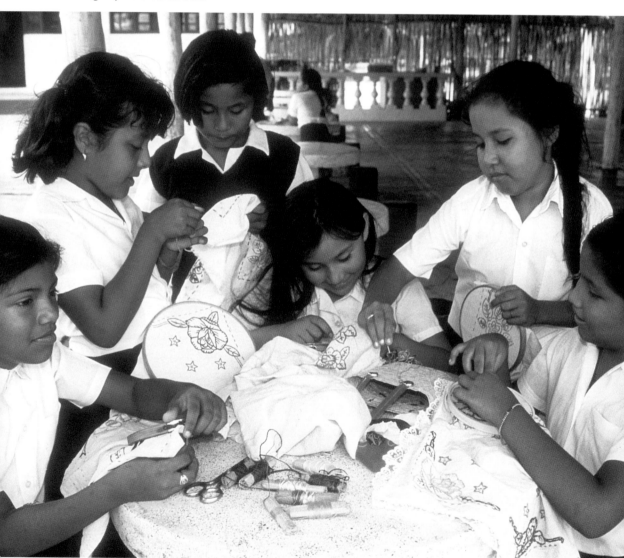

INUIT

The Inuit live in the Arctic, the northernmost region on the globe. This region stretches from Alaska into Canada.

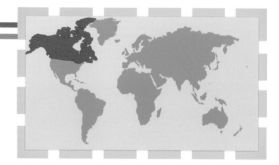

The Arctic is a kind of desert. But instead of sand, it has snow. And instead of hot weather, the Arctic has many months of bitter cold. During the long winter months, many Inuit practice their age-old art—carving in soapstone.

Soapstone is a soft, yet heavy stone found in this area. Traditionally, Inuit carvers like to re-create the animals that they hunt or their ancestors may have once captured. These animals include polar bears, caribou, seals, salmon, and whales. A carving may also show a hunting scene—a man spearing a seal or catching a salmon by jiggle, which is fishing through a hole in the ice.

No matter what the object is, Inuit carvers do not think of themselves as artists. It is their belief that the object is already inside the soapstone. All they are doing is chipping and filing away at the unneeded parts to expose the figure that already exists within the stone.

Above: An Inuit soapstone carver works on a sculpture.
Left: A finished soapstone carving.

BRAZIL

Brazil is the largest country in South America. It is the only country on the continent where Portuguese is the official language. That is because the Portuguese set up colonies in Brazil many years ago.

Over the centuries in Brazil, the Portuguese influence blended with African and native cultures. This blending can be heard in Brazil's famous bossa nova music and can be seen in its world-famous dance, the samba.

Rio de Janeiro is one of Brazil's largest and most important cities. Each year, a giant festival called Carnaval is held there. This festival is very similar to Mardi Gras, the celebration that takes place in New Orleans, Louisiana, every year. Carnaval is filled with nonstop music, food, and bright, elaborate costumes.

A young girl from Rio de Janeiro dresses in an elaborate costume for Carnaval.

During the months before Carnaval, many Brazilian children and their families spend days making the costumes they will wear. Some of these costumes are so detailed, they take the entire year to complete!

CHINA

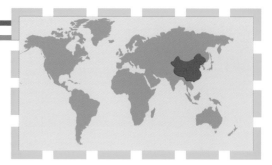

With almost a billion people, China is home to more than one fourth of the entire world's population.

While Chinese people do not all speak the same language, Mandarin Chinese is the one most widely spoken and written. This language does not have an alphabet or letters. Instead, people draw characters, or simple pictures to write their language. Each character represents an entire word or idea. There are over 3,000 characters used in Mandarin Chinese.

The art of writing these characters in a fine, careful style is called calligraphy. It is an art form that can be done in any alphabet. For the Chinese, writing in calligraphy is an ancient art that is highly prized and still practiced today.

Chinese calligraphers use ink and brushes instead of a pen to write each character. They may use calligraphy to copy a poem or a wise saying onto a scroll. A drawing to illustrate the saying or poem may also appear on the scroll, next to the calligraphy.

A young student practices the ancient art of calligraphy.

INDIA

India is a large country, with a huge population of over 780 million people. It is surrounded by three large bodies of water: the Arabian Sea to the west, the Indian Ocean to the south, and the Bay of Bengal to the east.

India has long been known for its very fine miniature paintings and highly detailed stonework. Artists have shown incredible scenes on tiny pieces of paper or stone. For their miniature paintings, they drew tiny scenes that showed as many as 50 men on horseback charging in a battle. Or, they drew a very detailed scene of a family that is surrounded by nature. Many miniature paintings were done to illustrate passages from famous Indian poems, like the Ramayana.

Above: A young boy prepares a slab of marble for stone inlay.
Inset: Small patterns are cut out of the marble to make room for different colored stone.

Artists today who follow these ancient traditions draw miniature pictures or do stone inlay that includes every little detail of a person, plant, or animal.

25

KENYA

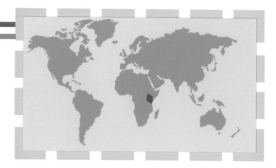

Kenya is on the east coast of Africa. Part of Kenya's border is on the Indian Ocean. The country is sandwiched between Ethiopia and Somalia to the north, and Tanzania to the south.

Kenya has large amounts of forest land. One of its products is the highly prized wood, mahogany. Kenyan sculptors often use this beautiful, dark wood to make their famous carvings. Kenyan woodcarvers may show the animals that are native to their land, such as the lion, zebra, elephant, or kudu (wild antelope). Or, they may carve out wood to resemble a human face. Many woodcarvers have learned their art from their parents. Woodcarving is a prized art form that is often handed down from one generation to the next within a family.

A Kenyan craftsman carves out a detailed border on a
wooden furniture piece.

CANADA

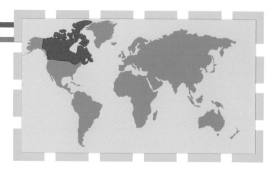

Canada is one of the largest countries in the world. Because most of it is so far north in North America, most people think of Canada as being covered in snow and ice most of the time. In fact, some parts of this country have a relatively mild winter.

Many parts of Canada hold winter festivals to celebrate the cold weather, snow, and ice. Ice sculpture is a common event at these festivals. Both professional sculptors and amateurs may be invited to create huge ice carvings. At the bigger festivals, famous Canadian sculptors use their chisels and other tools to carve into large blocks of ice. The sculpture may be a life-size animal or a full-size cabin. The finished ice sculptures are often decorated with tiny white lights to complete the scene and create a dramatic view at night.

A fire-breathing dragon ice sculpture is displayed at a Canadian winter festival.

ISRAEL

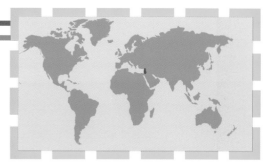

The land that is now called Israel has been occupied by many different people since biblical times. But the country of Israel, the official Jewish State, was only created in 1948.

The Israeli Philharmonic Orchestra is older than the country of Israel. The Philharmonic was formed in 1936. At that time, the area that is now Israel was known as Palestine. The orchestra was called the Palestine Symphony. Many of its members were famous German and Eastern European musicians. When Adolph Hitler and the Nazis came into power in Germany in the 1930s, many of these musicians escaped from the country. They went to Palestine to live and to continue practicing their art.

A young Israeli boy studies the violin with his teacher.

Children from Israel are encouraged to learn and master the traditional instruments of the orchestra, such as the piano, flute, violin, and French horn. Talented young musicians may be accepted into Israel's Junior Philharmonic. These lucky artists will often play in concerts right along with the Philharmonic's adult musicians.

GLOSSARY

depict To show a likeness of something through a painting, a drawing, or a sculpture.

immense Huge, very large in size.

immigrant A person born in one country but who leaves and lives permanently in another country.

indentation A scooped or hollowed-out part of something.

intricate Having many complicated parts.

merged Joined.

vibrantly Expressing a great deal of energy.

INDEX